# Table of Contents

# Spicy Grilled Chicken

**4 boneless skinless chicken breasts**
**2 tablespoons minced garlic**
**1 tablespoon salt**
**1 tablespoon red pepper flakes**
**2 teaspoons paprika**
**2 teaspoons black pepper**

**1.** Prepare grill for direct cooking over medium-high heat. Lightly score each chicken breast 3 or 4 times with knife.

**2.** Combine garlic, salt, red pepper flakes, paprika and black pepper in small shallow bowl. Coat both sides of chicken with garlic mixture.

**3.** Grill chicken 8 to 10 minutes or until chicken is no longer pink in center, turning once. *Makes 4 servings*

**Serving Suggestion:** Excellent served with rice pilaf.

# Beef and Pineapple Kabobs

**1 small onion, finely chopped**
**½ cup teriyaki sauce**
**1 boneless beef top sirloin or top round steak (about 1 pound),\* cut into ¼-inch-thick strips**
**16 pieces (1-inch cubes) fresh pineapple**
**1 can (8 ounces) water chestnuts, drained**

*\*Or substitute flank steak.*

**1.** Combine onion and teriyaki sauce in small bowl. Add beef strips; stir to coat.

**2.** Alternately thread beef strips (weaving back and forth), pineapple cubes and water chestnuts onto thin metal skewers.

**3.** Grill over medium coals 4 minutes or until meat is cooked through, turning once. Serve immediately. *Makes 4 servings*

# Baked Pasta Primavera Casserole

   1 jar (1 pound 10 ounces) RAGÚ® Old World Style® Pasta Sauce
   1 cup shredded part-skim mozzarella cheese (about 4 ounces)
   1 bag (16 ounces) frozen Italian-style vegetables, thawed
   1 box (16 ounces) ziti or penne pasta, cooked and drained
   ¼ cup grated Parmesan cheese

**1.** Preheat oven to 350°F. Combine Pasta Sauce and ½ cup mozzarella cheese in large bowl. Stir in vegetables and hot ziti.

**2.** Spoon pasta mixture into 2½-quart casserole; sprinkle with remaining ½ cup mozzarella cheese.

**3.** Bake, uncovered, 30 minutes or until heated through. Sprinkle with Parmesan cheese.                        *Makes 6 servings*

**Prep Time:** 20 minutes
**Cook Time:** 30 minutes

# Sweet and Salty Salmon

   4 skinless salmon fillets (6 ounces each)
   3 teaspoons brown sugar, divided
   4 slices bacon

**1.** Preheat oven to 350°F.

**2.** Place wire rack on top of baking sheet. Place salmon on wire rack; rub 1½ teaspoons brown sugar on top of salmon.

**3.** Cut each bacon slice crosswise into 2 pieces. Lay 2 bacon pieces over brown sugar on each salmon fillet, overlapping slightly. Sprinkle with remaining 1½ teaspoons brown sugar.

**4.** Bake 15 minutes or until bacon is crisp and salmon just begins to flake when tested with fork.                *Makes 4 servings*

# Tilapia with Spinach and Feta

1 teaspoon olive oil
1 clove garlic, minced
4 cups baby spinach
2 skinless fillets tilapia or other mild, medium-textured white
     fish (4 ounces each)
¼ teaspoon black pepper
2 ounces feta cheese, cut into 2 (3-inch) pieces

**1.** Preheat oven to 350°F. Spray baking sheet with nonstick cooking spray.

**2.** Heat oil in medium skillet over medium-low heat. Add garlic; cook and stir 2 minutes. *Do not burn.* Add spinach; cook just until wilted, stirring occasionally.

**3.** Arrange fillets on prepared baking sheet; sprinkle with pepper. Place one piece of cheese on each fillet; top with spinach mixture. Fold each fillet up and over filling; secure with toothpick.

**4.** Bake 20 minutes or until fish is firm and begins to flake easily when tested with fork. *Makes 2 servings*

# Stovetop Tuna Casserole

**10 cups cold water, divided**
**1 package (12 ounces) deluxe macaroni and cheese dinner with shell pasta**
**2 cups frozen peas**
**1 can (6 ounces) chunk white tuna**
**1 tablespoon butter**
**½ teaspoon black pepper**

**1.** Remove cheese sauce pouch from macaroni and cheese; set aside. Bring 6 cups cold water to a boil in large saucepan. Stir in pasta. Cook 6 to 8 minutes or until pasta is tender.

**2.** Meanwhile, bring 4 cups cold water to a boil in medium saucepan. Stir in peas. Cook 3 to 5 minutes or until tender.

**3.** Drain pasta and peas; return to saucepan. Stir in tuna, reserved cheese sauce pouch and butter until well blended. Sprinkle with black pepper.                    *Makes 4 servings*

**Variation:** Preheat oven to 350°F. Spray 8-inch baking dish with nonstick cooking spray. Spread tuna casserole mixture into prepared baking dish. Sprinkle with 1½ cups crushed potato chips or buttery round crackers. Bake 12 to 15 minutes or until topping is lightly browned.

**Tip:** Check your fridge for extra vegetables to toss into this quick casserole. Stir in ¼ to ½ cup with the peas. Try one peeled and finely chopped carrot, or finely chopped green onions, red onions, mushrooms or celery.

# Quick & Easy Pork Chops with Apples

 1 teaspoon olive oil
 4 bone-in pork chops, each ¾-inch thick
   Salt and black pepper
 2 to 3 apples, cored and sliced
 1½ cups dry white wine or apple juice

**1.** Heat oil in large nonstick skillet over medium heat. Brown pork chops on each side; season with salt and pepper.

**2.** Add apples and wine. Cover and cook 20 to 25 minutes or until pork is cooked through (165°F). Remove pork to platter; keep warm.

**3.** Bring apples and wine to a boil over medium-high heat. Cook 5 minutes or until liquid is reduced by half. Serve mixture over chops.                              *Makes 4 servings*

# Southwestern Enchiladas

 1 can (10 ounces) enchilada sauce, divided
 2 packages (about 6 ounces each) refrigerated fully cooked
   seasoned steak strips*
 4 (8-inch) flour tortillas
 ½ cup condensed nacho cheese soup, undiluted or chile-
   flavored pasteurized process cheese spread
 1½ cups (6 ounces) shredded Mexican cheese blend

*Fully cooked steak strips can be found in the refrigerated prepared meats section of the supermarket.*

**1.** Preheat oven to 350°F. Spread half of enchilada sauce in 9-inch square glass baking dish.

**2.** Arrange one fourth of steak down center of each tortilla. Top evenly with cheese soup. Roll up tortillas; place seam side down in prepared baking dish. Pour remaining enchilada sauce evenly over tortillas. Sprinkle with cheese blend.

**3.** Bake 20 to 25 minutes or until heated through.
                              *Makes 4 servings*

# Linguine with Easy Red Clam Sauce

- 1 tablespoon olive or vegetable oil
- 2 cloves garlic, minced
- 1½ cups PREGO® Traditional or Marinara Italian Sauce
- ¼ cup Chablis or other dry white wine
- 1 tablespoon chopped fresh parsley
- 2 cans (6½ ounces each) minced clams, undrained
- ½ package (8 ounces) linguine, cooked and drained (about 4 cups)
- Grated Parmesan cheese (optional)

**1.** Heat the oil in a 2-quart saucepan over medium heat. Add the garlic and cook until it is tender, stirring often.

**2.** Stir the Italian sauce, wine, parsley and clams and juice in the saucepan. Reduce the heat to low. Cover and cook for 10 minutes, stirring occasionally.

**3.** Serve the clam sauce over the linguine. Top with the cheese, if desired.

*Makes 4 servings*

**Kitchen Tip:** Angel hair or fettuccine can be substituted for the linguine in this recipe.

**Prep Time:** 20 minutes
**Cook Time:** 15 minutes
**Total Time:** 35 minutes

# Black Bean & Rice Stuffed Poblano Peppers

**2 large or 4 small poblano peppers**
**½ (15-ounce) can black beans, rinsed and drained**
**½ cup cooked brown rice**
**⅓ cup mild or medium chunky salsa**
**⅓ cup shredded Cheddar cheese or pepper Jack cheese, divided**

**1.** Preheat oven to 375°F. Lightly spray shallow baking pan with nonstick olive oil cooking spray.

**2.** Cut thin slice from one side of each pepper. Chop pepper slices; set aside. Cover remaining peppers with water in medium saucepan; bring to a boil. Boil 6 minutes. Drain and rinse with cold water; remove and discard seeds and membranes.

**3.** Stir beans, rice, salsa, chopped pepper and ¼ cup cheese in large bowl. Spoon into peppers, mounding mixture. Place peppers in prepared pan. Cover with foil.

**4.** Bake 12 to 15 minutes or until heated through. Sprinkle with remaining cheese. Bake 2 minutes or until cheese is melted.

*Makes 2 servings*

# Pork Tenderloin with Creamy Mustard Sauce

1 pound pork tenderloin
1 teaspoon vegetable oil
½ cup NESTLÉ® CARNATION® Evaporated Fat Free Milk
2 tablespoons Dijon mustard
2 to 3 green onions, sliced

CUT pork into 1-inch-thick slices. Place pork between two pieces of plastic wrap. Flatten to ¼-inch thickness using meat mallet or rolling pin. Season with salt and ground black pepper, if desired.

HEAT oil in large nonstick skillet over medium-high heat. Add *half* of the pork; cook on each side for 2 minutes or until browned and cooked through. Remove from skillet; set aside and keep warm. Repeat with *remaining* pork.

REDUCE heat to low. Add evaporated milk; stir to loosen brown bits from bottom of skillet. Stir in mustard and green onions. Return pork to skillet. Cook for 1 to 2 minutes or until sauce is slightly thickened, turning pork to coat.          *Makes 4 servings*

# Beef Stroganoff

1 can (10¾ ounces) condensed cream of mushroom soup, undiluted
1 cup (8 ounces) sour cream
1 package (1¼ ounces) dry onion soup mix
1½ pounds ground beef
1 cup peas
12 ounces wide egg noodles, cooked and drained

1. Combine mushroom soup, sour cream and onion soup mix in medium bowl; stir until well blended.

2. Brown beef 6 to 8 minutes in large skillet over medium-high heat, stirring to break up meat. Drain fat. Reduce heat to low.

3. Add soup mixture; stir until bubbly. Stir in peas; cook until heated through. Serve over noodles.          *Makes 6 servings*

# Cheesy Chicken & Broccoli Fettuccine

    1 to 2 tablespoons olive oil
    1 pound boneless skinless chicken breasts, cut into 1-inch pieces
    2 boxes (10 ounces each) frozen broccoli with cheese sauce,
        thawed
    1 package (12 ounces) fresh fettuccine, cooked and drained
      Salt and black pepper

**1.** Heat oil in large skillet over medium-high heat. Add chicken; cook and stir about 10 minutes or until cooked through.

**2.** Stir in broccoli and cheese sauce; heat until broccoli is crisp-tender.

**3.** Add fettuccine; stir to coat with cheese mixture. Season with salt and pepper.                    *Makes 8 servings*

**Note:** Fresh pasta cooks in a fraction of the time that boxed pasta cooks.

# Grilled Cuban Pork Chops with Pineapple

    1 packet (1.25 ounces) ORTEGA® Fajita Seasoning Mix
    ½ cup water
    4 pork chops (each ½ inch thick)
    1 can (20 ounces) sliced pineapple, drained

Blend seasoning mix and water in shallow baking dish. Add pork chops and turn to coat well. Marinate 15 minutes.

Preheat grill or broiler to high. Grill pork chops about 4 minutes. Turn and cook 4 minutes. Top pork chops with pineapple slices; grill 4 minutes longer. Serve pork chops with pineapple.
                              *Makes 4 servings*

**Tip:** Marinate a small pork tenderloin in the fajita seasoning mixture, then grill it over high heat about 15 minutes. Slice and serve with grilled pineapple.

**Prep Time:** 15 minutes

# Easy Santa Fe Style Stuffed Peppers

**1 cup MINUTE® Brown Rice, uncooked**
   **Nonstick cooking spray**
**1 pound lean ground beef***
**1 package (10 ounces) frozen whole-kernel corn**
**1½ cups chunky salsa**
   **4 large red bell peppers, tops and seeds removed****
**1 cup Colby and Monterey Jack cheese, shredded**

*Or substitute ground turkey.*
**Or substitute green, yellow or orange bell peppers.*

Prepare rice according to package directions.

Preheat oven to 425°F.

Spray large nonstick skillet with nonstick cooking spray. Add beef; brown over medium heat. Drain excess fat. Stir in corn, salsa and rice.

Pierce bell peppers with fork or sharp knife; place in baking dish. Fill peppers with meat mixture. Cover with foil.

Bake 20 minutes. Uncover. Sprinkle with cheese before serving.

*Makes 4 servings*

**Tip:** If softer peppers are desired, reduce the oven temperature to 375°F and cook the filled peppers, covered, for 1 hour.

# Oriental Vegetables and Ham

    **2 cups chicken broth**
    **1 pound frozen stir-fry vegetables**
    **1 teaspoon sesame oil**
    **4 ounces thinly sliced ham, cut into ½-inch squares**
    **2 cups uncooked instant white long-grain rice**
      **Soy sauce (optional)**

1. Place broth, vegetables and sesame oil in large saucepan; bring to a boil over high heat. Remove from heat; stir in ham and rice. Cover and let stand 5 minutes.

2. Serve with soy sauce, if desired.      *Makes 4 servings*

**Variation:** You can substitute ¾ pound cooked chicken for the ham.

# Baked Cod with Tomatoes and Olives

    **1 pound cod fillets (about 4 fillets), cut into 2-inch pieces**
      **Salt and black pepper**
    **1 can (about 14 ounces) diced Italian-style tomatoes, drained**
    **2 tablespoons chopped pitted black olives**
    **1 teaspoon minced garlic**
    **2 tablespoons chopped fresh parsley**

1. Preheat oven to 400°F. Spray 13×9-inch baking dish with nonstick olive oil cooking spray. Arrange cod in pan; season with salt and pepper.

2. Combine tomatoes, olives and garlic in medium bowl. Spoon over fish.

3. Bake 20 minutes or until fish flakes when tested with a fork. Sprinkle with parsley.      *Makes 4 servings*

**Serving Suggestion:** Spread French bread with softened butter, sprinkle with paprika and oregano. Broil until lightly toasted; serve with baked cod.

# Honey Lime-Glazed Chicken

1 whole chicken, quartered (about 3 pounds) or
    3 pounds chicken parts
⅓ cup honey
2 tablespoons lime juice
1 tablespoon plus 1½ teaspoons soy sauce
3 cups hot cooked thin noodles (3½ ounces uncooked)

**1.** Preheat oven to 375°F. Arrange chicken, skin side up, in single layer in shallow casserole dish or 11×7-inch baking dish.

**2.** Combine honey, lime juice and soy sauce in small bowl; mix well. Brush half of honey mixture over chicken.

**3.** Bake 15 minutes. Brush remaining honey mixture over chicken. Bake 10 to 15 minutes or until cooked through (180°F). Transfer to serving platter. Serve with noodles. *Makes 4 servings*

# Sweet and Sour Beef

1 pound ground beef
1 small onion, thinly sliced
2 teaspoons minced fresh ginger
1 package (16 ounces) frozen Asian-style vegetables
6 to 8 tablespoons bottled sweet and sour sauce or sauce from
    vegetable mix
  Hot cooked rice

**1.** Brown beef, onion and ginger 6 to 8 minutes in large skillet over medium-high heat, stirring to break up meat. Drain fat.

**2.** Stir in frozen vegetables and sauce. Cover; cook and stir 6 to 8 minutes or until vegetables are heated through. Serve over rice. *Makes 4 servings*

**Serving Suggestion:** Serve with sliced Asian pears.

# Rigatoni à la Vodka

   1 pound ground beef
   1 jar (26 ounces) prepared pasta sauce
   1½ cups 3-cheese pasta sauce
   4 cups (16 ounces) shredded mozzarella and Cheddar cheese blend, divided
   6 tablespoons vodka
   12 ounces rigatoni pasta, cooked and drained

1. Preheat oven to 350°F. Spray 3-quart casserole with nonstick cooking spray.

2. Brown beef 6 to 8 minutes in medium skillet over medium-high heat, stirring to break up meat. Drain fat. Add pasta sauces, 2 cups cheese and vodka; cook and stir until heated through.

3. Place cooked pasta in prepared casserole. Pour vodka sauce evenly over pasta; sprinkle with remaining 2 cups cheese.

4. Bake 15 minutes or until cheese is melted.

*Makes 4 servings*

# 15-Minute Chicken and Broccoli Risotto

   1 tablespoon vegetable oil
   1 small onion, chopped
   2 packages (about 9 ounces each) ready-to-serve yellow rice
   2 cups frozen chopped broccoli
   1 package (about 6 ounces) refrigerated fully cooked chicken breast strips, cut into pieces
   ½ cup chicken broth or water
   Sliced almonds (optional)

1. Heat oil in large skillet over medium-high heat. Add onion; cook and stir 3 minutes or until translucent. Knead rice in bag. Add rice, broccoli, chicken and broth to skillet.

2. Cover; cook 6 to 8 minutes or until heated through, stirring occasionally. Garnish with almonds. *Makes 4 servings*

# Cucumber Ranch Steaks

**4 beef shoulder center steaks (Ranch Steak), cut ¾ inch thick (about 5 ounces each)**
**½ cup finely chopped seeded cucumber**
**¼ cup prepared ranch dressing**
**1 tablespoon garlic-pepper seasoning**
**1 small tomato, seeded, diced (optional)**

1. Combine cucumber and dressing in small bowl. Set aside.

2. Press garlic-pepper seasoning evenly onto beef steaks. Place steaks on grid over medium, ash-covered coals. Grill, covered, 9 to 11 minutes (over medium heat on preheated gas grill, covered, 8 to 11 minutes) for medium rare (145°F) to medium (160°F) doneness, turning occasionally.

3. Serve steaks with cucumber sauce. Garnish with tomato, if desired. *Makes 4 servings*

**Cook's Tip:** To easily seed a cucumber, cut it lengthwise in half and use the tip of a teaspoon to scrape out the seeds. European or English greenhouse-grown cucumbers, now available in many supermarkets, are virtually seedless.

**Prep and Cook Time:** 25 to 30 minutes

Favorite recipe from **Courtesy The Beef Checkoff**

## ACKNOWLEDGMENTS

The publisher would like to thank the companies and organizations listed below for the use of their recipes and photographs in this publication.

The Beef Checkoff

Campbell Soup Company

Nestlé USA

Ortega®, A Division of B&G Foods, Inc.

Riviana Foods Inc.

Unilever